TEENAGE MELANCHOLY

teenage melancholy

francesca joanna

Francesca Joanna Martin

teenage melancholy copyright © 2021 by Francesca Joanna Martin

All rights reserved. No part of this book may be reproduced in any manner whatsoever without written permission except in the case of brief quotations embodied in critical articles and reviews.

ISBN: 978-0-578-90805-2

Illustrations by Francesca Joanna Martin

First Printing, 2021

*for those who have endured
teenage melancholy.*

*everything will be okay,
because you are strong.*

AUTHOR'S NOTE

welcome to my first collection of poetry.

i first want to thank you for taking the time to read this work of mine, which was composed from the bottom of my heart.

i would also like to disclose the background of my inspiration for this poetry collection and my wish for you as you read these poems.

when i first opened up a poetry book and read the first page, i instantly fell in love with poetry. until then, i started buying and reading more poetry books and collections, which can explain the tons stacking up on my bookshelf.

the sole reason why i love poetry is because i feel a sense of being genuinely understood and heard regarding any circumstance when reading any poetry book. this can be a sad and downhearted one or even a happy and uplifting one. i overall feel peace and most importantly, alleviation from sufferings or troubles.

after reading many poems, i was inspired to

give writing poetry a try. i then constructed my very first poem out of my emotions and feelings and became motivated to write many more. it was at that time when *teenage melancholy* was put together.

all these poems inside of this collection come from real-life (messy) situations and phases i have encountered during my teenage years, including painful relationships and overwhelming mental health conditions. however, they do have a message for those who have encountered similar situations as me:

from hurtful and despairing events, we often feel discouraged, hopeless, and melancholic. but in the end, these events will only awaken you and cause you to take action of learning the best from the worst.

so, i want you, the reader, to feel seen and heard, especially during your lowest times.
there is always light at the end of the tunnel.

let these poems be your listeners.

- francesca joanna

PHASES

I. THE DARK	1
heartbreak	3
melancholy	43
mentality	61
II. THE FOG	77
adoration	79
lessons	109
III. THE LIGHT	125
confrontation	127
relief	157

I

THE DARK

heartbreak

this is how a heart can be broken

do not come to me
if you just want a taste
of how it feels like
to be handled with care

and just dip right after.

because then,
you will end up
breaking *my fragile heart.*

conquest

the words you shared with me,
the compliments you gave me,

i just can't help but think
how they made me feel
so special.

so adored,
so loved.

but
little did my young self know,
there was someone else
you also gave them to
at the same damn time.

everything comes to an end

you asked me
what my biggest fear was.

i said losing you.

how ironic.

cherish

in all honesty,
i always become hesitant
to get a new phone.

the truth is,
i don't want my only memories
that i have left of you
to go to waste.

i should've known

i guess i fell in love
with my first impression of you.

not for who you really are
behind that mask.

i overslept today

4:18pm.

as my dog's bark awakens me,
i check the time on my phone.

it saddens me
how i've wasted
most of my day.

just how i've wasted
most of my time
falling head over heels
for someone like you.

walking away

i can't seem to fathom
why differences
can play a huge factor
in such serious consequences.

the fucked up part is that
people may hold you against them.

they won't quite understand
that you want different things
for your own well-being.

and it's not being selfish,
it's simply putting
your pride and self-worth first.
only you know what's best for you.

and so you part ways.

regrets

last night,
i went through drafts of texts
that i never hit send to you.

because i realized that
while you were still mine,
you would've at least known
and wouldn't have been oblivious
about how i really felt for you.

it maybe would've kept you
from leaving.

but there's no damn rewind button
to go back in time.

insecurities

sometimes
i don't even bother
to go on my phone
and scroll on it.

because i know
that i'll just see you

with her.

ghosting

i don't know why
i felt upset when
you didn't respond.

instead,
i should've never
responded to you
in the first place.

i would've been thriving
independently
without the knowledge
of your existence.

hypocrisy

it really makes one look foolish
when they tell you
they are there for you.

the typical words you hear from them include,
but are not limited to,
is everything okay?
just wanted to check in on you.

and when the actual moment comes
when you need them,
all those words
are just plain bullshit.

and the worse thing
they can tell you after is,
your problems aren't my responsibilities.

b&w

my life was vibrant
before i met you.

then we met
and it began to grow dim.

and now that you're gone,
it's colorless.

this is how it feels like to be used

i showed you a side
that not much people have seen of me.

i told you how i felt
because i didn't want to hold my feelings in.

i offered my sweet, kind, and generous soul
to show you how much i truly cared.

but still,
you took a part of me
and left.

triggered

i never want to go out
to movie theaters,
candlelight dinners,
the beaches to watch sunsets,
or the rooftops to look at views.

even if those are my favorite go-to places.

because then,
i'm reminded that
i can never go there with you.

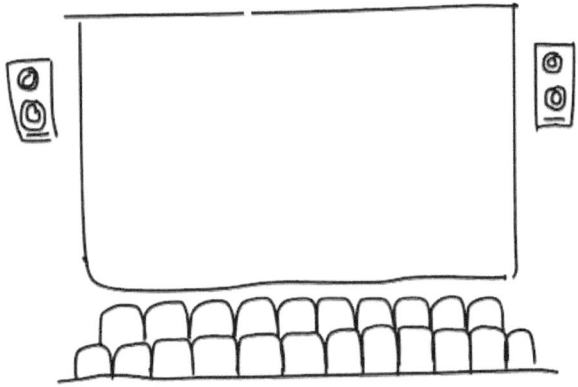

impatient

this time
it really hurt
because before
i could even show you
what i could offer

you left
because you wanted it that instant
with a snap of a finger

and thought time
was unnecessary and boring.

ruined

we already had
something special going on,
or at least in my opinion.

but you just had
to fuck it up.

scribbling gibberish
all over the promising house
we were building.

rent

thank you for making me feel
like a library book.

something you needed
for your favor
but returned
once you were finished.

smh.

so many people
warned me about you.

but i was too busy
being drawn
to the fake persona
you displayed.

what you used
to conceal your ugliness.

hollow

you're different.

the last lie i heard from you.

what your words did to me

it was just in the heat of the moment
is another way of saying,
can you simply just forget
all the stupid shit i said
even though it has left
a permanent speck
inside your head?

betrayal

one of the most painful things
i've ever experienced
was being attentive to people
who weren't even worth it
this whole time.

i felt the need to provide them
support, sincerity, and friendship,

only to be stabbed in the back.

stain

i'm permanently bruised.

because there's still a fraction of me
that remembers very clearly

the way you flipped out when i disagreed for once.
the way you abused me with your words.
the way you forgot i was human too.

ignorance

you say that
i'm using my mental health
as a dear excuse.
as a *sob story*.

you act as if
i asked for this state of mind.

you act as if
i asked to suffer in this way.

maybe you don't truly know me.

maybe we're just perfect strangers.

the aftermath of confessing our feelings to each other

you were like ice.

you melted away
once the intense heat
rose between us.

deceitful

you told me
you wanted to show me
true love.

and when you tried to
i only fell
out of it.

moving on

i'll never measure up
to the new girl you started seeing.

she's taller,
more outgoing,
more popular.

so it's time for me to let go of
something ridiculous
that'll never happen.

goodbye

i rarely give
second chances.

yet,
i was optimistic
for the both of us.

i thought
you could change for me.

i thought
you could learn from your mistakes.

but i was wrong.
stupid.
and young.

i made the mistake
of letting you in.

twice.

and so this is my
final *goodbye.*

alone again

february 14, 12:00am.

it's valentine's day.

just another day
to get through.

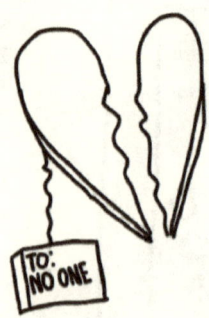

leaving all the pain behind

let's run away
from this heartbreaking city.

nostalgic

it's been a while
since we've last talked or seen each other.

but my provoking little mind
still wonders
what you're up to now.

it also wonders
if you ever think about me too.
even if it was just once.

or perhaps,
you've already forgotten about me.
threw all the memories of me away in the trash.

the demons inside of me

the monsters aren't living
under my bed.

they are instead
wandering around
inside my head
painting pictures
again and again
of your impractical return.

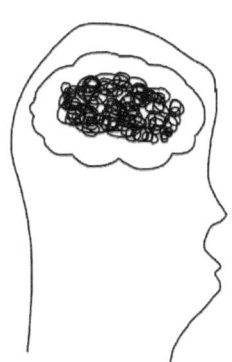

it slipped out of my mind for a second

i received some great news today.

i was about to send you a text,
but i totally forgot

we aren't cool anymore.

it's the small things that remind me of us.

i accidentally dropped
my favorite coffee mug
on the floor this morning.

and that was just like us.

broken and can never be
repaired.

best friend always knows best

oh how it was such a coincidence
when my best friend told me,
i understand you're into him now,
but when it doesn't work out,
i'll be here for you
and take you out for ice cream.

and that's exactly
what ended up happening.

threats

it's quite frightening
when you've let someone
enter your life
and gave them a pass
to see the real you

but they're not in your life
anymore.

because they're somewhere out there
aware of *your deepest secrets and fears.*

when all is said and done

heart broke
at seventeen.

melancholy

the reality

i don't listen to sad music
just because
everyone else does.

i listen to it
because deep down
i'm really not okay.

these songs,
these words,
these lyrics,

are all that hear me out
in a way that
nobody else ever does.

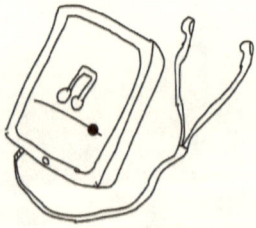

insomnia: because of my melancholic mood

3:29am.

i'm not that tired
so i'm going to listen
to that playlist
that makes me contemplate
and cry
at this hour.

embarrassment

how do i open up
to my therapist

and tell her the reason
why i'm feeling sad
is because of you

without sounding like
a fool?

when i can't relate

i went to work today
and my co-workers
were all discussing
their love lives.

i immediately felt left out
since i don't have
too much relation
with that.

in my head

i've always thought
falling in love
and meeting the right person
to do it with
was easy.

they simply come to you
and show up.

it can also be
that i'm still too young,
which is reasonable.

but i always recall this thought
every time i see my peers fulfilling it,

which makes me start
to doubt it even more.

francesca joanna | 49

same old, same old

at this point,
i'm getting used to
the loneliness.

irony

i find it kind of funny
how rom-coms
are one of my favorite movie genres.

because i never had the chance
to experience what i'm watching
on the screens.

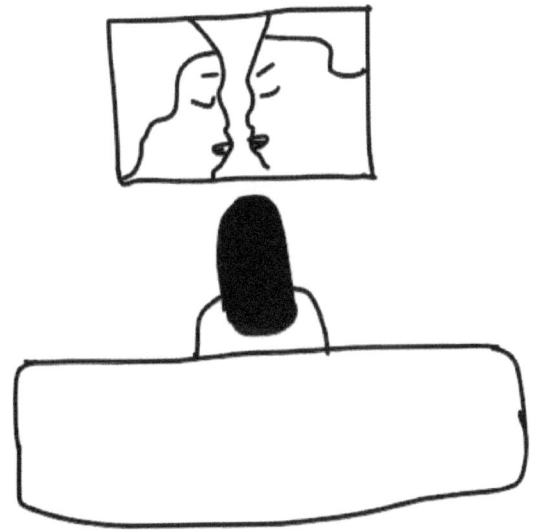

worries

i am sitting in my bedroom
contemplating about my future.

it's been too damn long
since i've been watching movies,
dining in at restaurants,
and going on these road trips
all by myself.

how do i expect
to eventually
share my heart
with someone
if i've been single
for the majority of my life?

teen

most people have told me,
high school was such a fun experience, i loved it.
savor it while you can because you'll miss it.

but i've spent most of my high school years
living through the pains and struggles of:

anxiety,
depression,
toxicity,
loneliness,
and exclusion.

would you look at that.

silenced

i feel so lonely.

they don't want
to listen to me.

it's like my whole voice
is on mute.

and the unmute button
is broken and disabled.

and the only person i have
is *me, myself, and i.*

empathy

let these poems
be the ones that hear you out
during your vulnerable times.

empty

i might already
have everything.

i mean…
i have my family,
friends,
education,
passion for music,
and love for poetry.

why do i still find myself
in miserable conditions?

i still feel deserted.

i need company.

whenever i feel depressed and lonely,
i always just wish to flee
the current place i'm at
and be with the people close to me
who would make me laugh
and give me at least
a small sense of happiness.

i want to have a breath of fresh air
and become distracted
in the best way possible.

the worse thing i'd want to do
is stay in a place
where the weather is fogged up and grey
and be alone
with nobody's shoulder to lean on.

even just thinking about it
makes me gloomy.

baggage

it's really hard
when you're experiencing rough times
and everyone close to you
has their own shit to deal with.

and the crappy thing about it is that
you might look selfish
and feel like a burden,
but your feelings are
inevitably eating you up.

so you need to just
endure it yourself.

neglected.

it's another day
i feel unloved and uncared for.
friendless and abandoned,
with no one to reach out to.

no one who dares to listen
to what the fuck i'm feeling
during this despondent time.

mentality

fuck you, anxiety.

it's frustrating
how we can't control
how we feel
or what we have.

we are naturally born
with distinctive personalities and mental states.

we blossom
with different experiences and memories.

each one of us is different.

however,
we become unsatisfied and unfortunate
with the feelings we come across.

and mine
is being stuck
in the deep hole
of *anxiety.*

delicate

my emotions are continuously
riding on a roller coaster.

i can never get a grip on them.

for instance,
i cry a lot.

i'm too sensitive.

even over the smallest things.
i can't help it.

and it irks me
because people who cannot relate
would say i'm a *crybaby*.

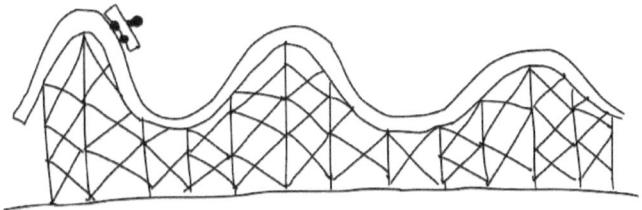

powerful mind of mine

there's one part in my body
that speaks so loud.

my mind,
along with the thoughts
and feelings it carries,
is just so loud.

no matter how hard i try
to silence it
for just a moment,
it doesn't work.

now you may ask,
why would you ever want to silence your mind?

that's because inside of it
are negative,
overthinking,
and fearful energies.

the thoughts that
awaken my anxiety.

the ones that keep me up at night
and disturb me.

the ones that make me feel like
i have nothing to offer.

but,
i'd like to hope and think
that there's a special
someone out there
who can magically
silence them.

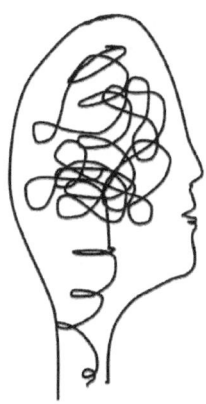

sequence

each time i start to love myself again,
a couple of days later,
i go back to square one
only to *hate* myself again.

unfair

do you ever just sit and wonder
what you've done
to deserve such a
wretched mindset?

stung

it's pretty rare for me
to have confidence within myself.

but there are some good days,
where i finally feel
successful and content
for something i believe i achieved.

regardless,
it sucks how
there's still people out there
who will shit on your self-esteem
and have a piece of criticism or judgement
to give you.

there goes my confidence.

not my cup of tea

i've always heard
that taking
deep long breaths
reduce your stress.

but in all honesty,
that never really works
for me.

it's either
i need more practice
on that

or my anxiety levels
are always unavoidably
too fucking high
no matter what.

courtesy

have you ever been
at an event
that you were
forced to attend

and just sat there
uncomfortable as fuck?

yet
there you were
maintaining that
fake smile.

this is how i feel like in public

i'm such an overthinker.
i always care too much
about what others say of me.

it's like these people
also have eyes and ears
on their backs.

watching and judging
my every move
from left and right.

overcoming anxiety

i can remember the day
when i cried to my parents
and to my friends.

i wanted to surrender.

i was ready
to allow my negative emotions
to get the best of me.

it didn't help
how people around me
didn't notice.
but they can't read my mind,
so i don't blame them.

it honestly felt like
i was trapped
in a whole different world
where misery
dominates the people.

however,
in another world,
people are stable and satisfied,
with the joy you get when
you're surrounded by puppies.

but,
i am now
gradually working my way
towards that blissful world.

here's a challenging question

i'm not sure what's better:

perfection and excelling

or

vulnerability and growing?

II

THE FOG

adoration

i hope i find you soon

there are some days
i picture ourselves
finding each other

fulfilling everything
i imagined
in my own mind.

maybe in another universe

i just wish
i can tell you
face to face,
i never felt this way for anyone else, but ONLY you.

my ideal day

on bright sunny days,
i walk to the local cafe
located in my neighborhood.

and who knows,
maybe
i'll run into you.

i don't want to wake up

you're already up there.
as big as these tall pine trees.

yet here i am,
the grass that lies on the ground.

just a young simple teenage girl,
living in a dream to be with you.

hoping that one day,
these feelings would somehow
be *reciprocated.*

i'll just go on a walk instead.

i used to take naps a lot.

but i stopped that habit
so i'd decrease the chances
of having another dream of you.

in denial

it's so absurd
how i'm falling in love
with someone
who doesn't even know
that i exist.

my illogical visions

i don't know
if i want these dreams in my sleep
to be real or not.

because at least in some of them
i'm living in a world
where there's
a you and me.

insomnia: caught in a daze

3:36am.

i literally spend
most nights
thinking about you.

simpleminded

it's stupid.

i'm over here
thinking that
i'm the one for you.

but you're already
in someone else's arms
with this thought

nowhere near
your mind.

fantasy

if my friends were to describe me,
they'd say i'm a *hopeless romantic.*

because
i'm prone to the thought
that love is exquisite
when you eventually meet
the one.

unnoticed

the only thing that i'll have
to be close to you
is the screen i'm looking at.

your ghost

today,
i got ready for once.

i made an actual effort
to curl my hair,
apply on some makeup,
and display a bright aura.

the only thing that was missing
was *your presence.*

today, i went on an afternoon hike.

5:34pm.

sunsets are beautiful
just like you.

obstacles

oh how i wish nervousness
was never a thing.

because i would've had the courage
to tell you how i feel
and lay by your side
long ago.

this is for you

no matter if we never talk,
i still made this playlist for you.
i still sang these songs for you.
i still wrote these poems for you.

i invested
most of my free time
doing these things
for you.

cravings

i want to be the muse
in the songs you write.

i want to be the muse
in the paintings you paint.

i want to be the muse
in the drawings you draw.

i want to be
a part of your *art*.

insomnia: why i started taking melatonin

5:12am.

i cannot sleep.
and it's not the two cups of coffee
i drank earlier.

it's the recurring thought
of you.

timid

i really want to be with you,
but i'm just not bold enough.

i'm afraid.

the overwhelming
and doubtful thoughts
come rushing through
my head and heart.

simpleminded (again)

i'm writing these romantic poems
specifically for you,

a person
who will *never* read them.

fictional

if genies and their magic were real,
you'd definitely be on my wish list.

too bad it doesn't work like that.

late nights

2:16am.

the best vibe right now
would be driving through the city in downtown
with the windows rolled down
and your hand cupping my face.

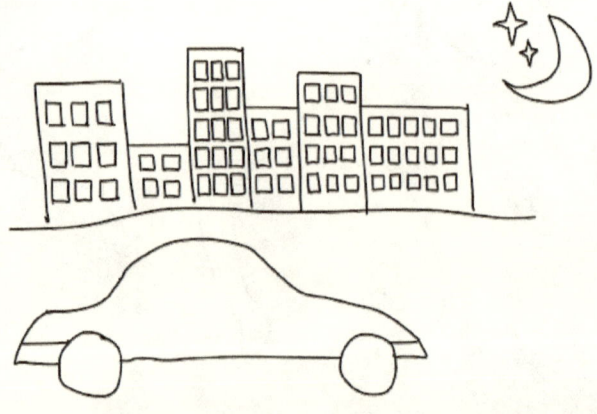

paradise

your skin
pushed on my skin
feels like *heaven.*

paris

i haven't traveled very much,
but there's one specific place
that i would die to visit.

and that's paris.

imagine our adolescent selves
intertwining
and being so infatuated
in the so-called

picturesque
and most romantic city.

patience

i'm waiting for the one
who can prove his loyalty and worthiness,
stay with me through thick and thin,
be attracted to my quirky humor,
admire all my passions,
respect my decisions,
treat me right,

and last but not least,
show me what it means
to be *genuinely loved.*

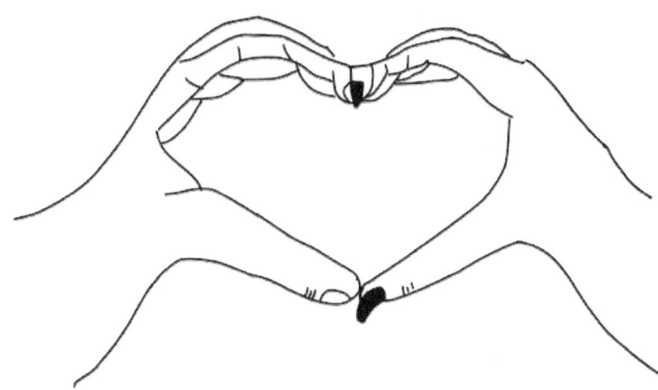

to my soulmate: when we meet.

*on a warm summer day
in los angeles.*

june 14, 12:23pm.

we have brunch together
on sunset boulevard.

we exchange our favorite
hobbies and interests
and talk about our families.

the conversation goes on,
as you admire
the sundress i'm wearing.

everything is perfect.
we connect so well.

2:38pm.

we stroll around echo park,

deciding to ride boats
on the shimmering lake.

you steer the wheel
on one hand
as we both pedal.

your other hand
gently touches mine,
signaling to hold it.

we both chuckle
and smile at each other.

for once,
i feel something
that i've never felt before.

6:56pm.

you drive me home,
escorting me
to my doorstep.

my parents unexpectedly

come outside,
which sparks the
nervousness within me.

they approach you,
introduce themselves,
and ask you more
about yourself.

their concerned faces
fade away
and smiles appear,
with faces of satisfaction.

they say goodbye,
heading back inside.

and that's when we kiss.

and that's when i know
it's the *best day of my life.*

lessons

learn

somehow i thank you
for fucking me over.

because now,
i don't just go around
donating my trust.

now,
i'm more observant.

now,
i can tell who's a phony.

now,
i know who just aims
to take advantage of me.

so thank you for that.

bear with the pain

the authentic form of poetry
stems from agony.

realizations

i'm done
being too nice
and lenient.

all i ever did
was let shit slip
and forgive
and forget.

but it's time i be cautious,
watching out for the red flags
the second i see them.

bffs

i will accept
the impossibility
of finally finding a boy
who sees me for me.

at least
i am lucky enough
to have my best friend
who constantly reminds me
of my worth.

manifestation

when i make mistakes
and things don't go the way
i thought they'd go,

i tend to live in the past.

the failure remains in my head.

but,
i learned to stop focusing
on something i cannot change

and instead
look forward
and work towards
what i aspire to happen.

i pray.
i journal.
i create vision boards.
i light up a fresh scented candle to summon positivity.
i listen to my euphoric playlist.

i try my absolute best
to brush off the doubts.

productivity

rather than sitting there
waiting for a calling

how about you stand up
and strive to *create yourself.*

puzzled

sometimes i wonder
if the actions i take
and the choices i make
are rightfully flawed.

because i find myself
in messy situations
where people expect
different from me.

is it me,
or is this world
filled with inevitable toxicity?

life lesson

being turned down hurts.

of course.

i thought i'd be a big person
and be capable of taking it well.

i never thought
i can feel so blue
and allow a single decision
to define me as a whole.

but if there's one important lesson
that i've ever learned,

it's never allowing
one person or thing
screw up what you've already
put on the table.

you need to remember
all the hard work you contributed.

all the shit you went through
to be the person you are today.

because all that
is what really defines you.

not the decision
that others made
to turn your hardworking self
down.

it's simply *their loss.*

the end

at least your departure
opened up my eyes
after being blinded
by the fantasies i held on to
for what we could've been.

proof

i'm going to take you leaving
as a crystal clear sign for us
not being meant for each other.

the old me

when i was younger,
i would always allow people
to step on me
without putting a foot down.

there were people
who disliked me.

people who thought
i needed to be better,
both physically
and mentally.

people who thought
i was just this meek
and naive person.

but,
ages have passed
and i've gone through
even more intense struggles
only to become stronger

to take risks
and learn more
valuable lessons.

i can only hope
that from now on,
i continue on this path
as i grow older
and flourish
the old me.

III

THE LIGHT

confrontation

better without you

when you first left,
i honestly still wanted you
to view my posts.

see what i'm doing now
without your negative energy pulling me down.

see how i'm progressing
and giving zero fucks about you.

but as time passed,
that feeling disappeared.

because i realized it was just pathetic.
something you are yourself.

why we disconnected.

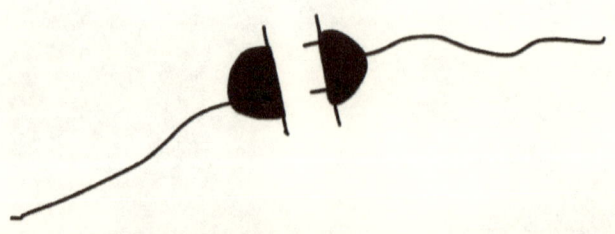

absent

yes,
push me away.

keep saying these things
in the heat of the moment.

keep being impulsive.

because in time
when you decompress,

you'll be left with wounds
that'll never heal.

you'll wish
i was *still present.*

to save yourself some time

if you're now going to
shoot your shot at her,

might as well
copy and paste
from your other texts.

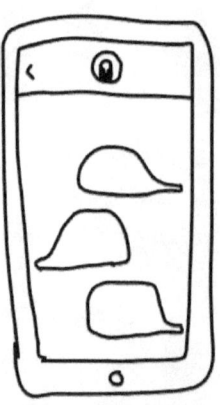

familiar games

please don't feel offended
if i say *no*.

because i can already see
right through you.

i know it's unworthy.

how?

because i've already seen this before.

isolation

there's nothing that makes me
more uncomfortable
than being in a room
crowded with people.

i like my space.
i like my small circle.
i like being able to breathe.

so pardon me
if i'm being
antisocial.

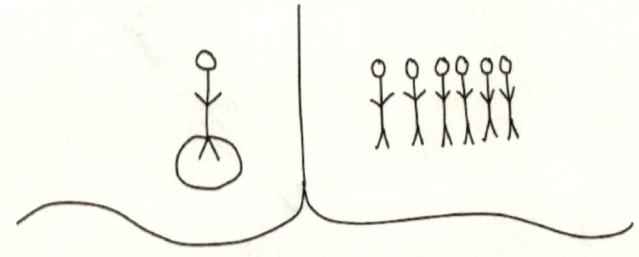

when you told me i had *the worse response game*

i'm sorry
for not replying as fast
as you wanted me to.

but i'm not sorry
for having a life
outside of all this social media too.

fulfilling
my other obligations.
my priorities.
my work.

vengeance

of course
i'm pissed at those
who did me dirty.

but i'm not going to
bother getting back.

it's a waste of energy.

just how i wasted time
minding them.

but,
i am going to hope
they at least mature.

persuasion

i'm very curious.

my mind is full of
questions and uncertainty.

what were you told
that made me look
like a demon to you?

perhaps,
it was the evil power
of *brainwashing*.

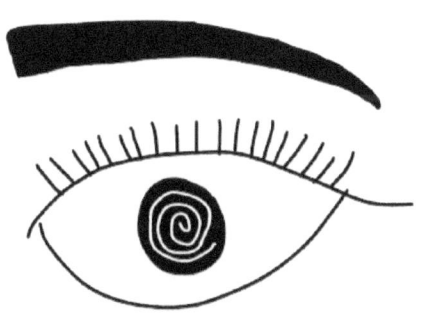

greed

i don't value materials
over actions.

i'm always grateful
for what's being
presented onto me.

but what i really care about
first and foremost,
is how i'm being treated
and cared for.

i need to be sure
that i form
healthy relationships
that will last
and not just contribute
to another
heartache.

accuracy

never give permission
for someone
to jump to conclusions
and accuse you
for shit you didn't do.

if that happens,
fucking set the record straight
and get their facts right.

i wish you knew better

are you not seeing
or hearing this?

it kind of hurts
how someone as warm as you
is siding with the wrong person.

i would've loved to see neutrality.

the give and take

it's okay to love someone.

it's okay to open up to them
and give them your everything.

but it's never okay
to control them.

it's never okay
to cross their boundaries.

and it's definitely not okay
to force them into something
they don't want.

set your limits.

don't get comfortable
being superior to them.

you don't want
the ones you love
to vanish.

i'm not surprised, just sorry for the others.

and so he moves on
quickly after two days
to another naive girl
after the previous one
doesn't work out.

his usual routine.

everything and anything

stop trying to hold on
just because you find
one thing
intriguing about me.

you need to embrace
the entirety of my attributes.

draining

you think you're always right

and i'm sick of it.

get your shit together

maybe it wouldn't have to end like this if you'd:

1. stop categorizing yourself as an angel.

2. stop denying your imperfections.

3. stop your tendency of instigating.

4. stop being aggressive when things didn't go your way.

5. stop adding fuel to the fire.

i can state many reasons
because you instantly became
a shadow that faded away from my life.

toxic

please stop
crawling back to me.

we both know
you're no good
for my health.

inconsistency

you own this habit

of switching up
like the seasons.

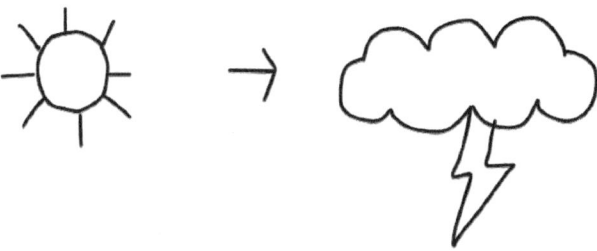

worthwhile

i don't care
if you're going to make me feel
all these butterflies and passions
only for a while.

i will only take the chance
if it will be consistent
or even *forever.*

dedication

if you aren't available at the moment,
they would automatically take the opportunity
to wait for you.

they wouldn't go wandering around
looking for another to keep them company
during the times you can't.

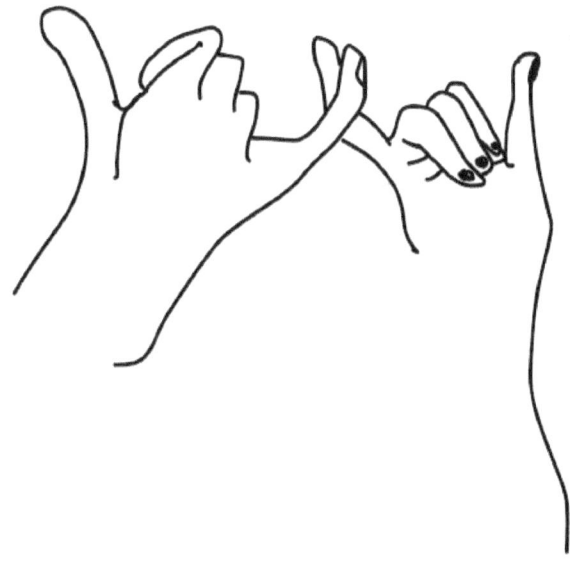

keep your distance

i get that we're close,
but i shouldn't feel obligated
to disclose all the information
that goes on in my life to you.

i need my space
in order to feel comfortable
in our relationship.

awake

i kind of want you
to experience
someone walking out of your life
very instantly
after an incident you caused.

that way
you'll think to yourself,
why does this seem so familiar?

you'll maybe then realize
that it was always you in the wrong.

taken for granted

i hope you feel mesmerized
when you get to know her.

i hope you feel like she's enough
when you get to know her.

because i tried giving you my all,
but it sadly didn't meet
your expectations.

shallow

a couple of my concerns:

what if
i didn't wear makeup on my lazy days?

what if
i didn't style my hair today?

what if
i didn't dress like it was a hot summer day?

would you still see me the same?

you can't stay here

you still want to be
a part of my life.

but i'm not sure
i can tolerate that

after the true colors of bitterness
i just witnessed from you.

this is who i am. are you willing to accept me?

i am never going to transform myself
just to please you.

just to make me feel like
i'm sufficient enough for you.

just to fit your definition
of *perfect*.

even if you feel like
you aren't sufficient enough for me
because i'm not one to judge either.

if you don't like who i am as a person,
then what are you really here for?

why do you keep
lingering around?

sentimental

i don't want to be known
just because of someone else's success.

for something i didn't accomplish.

i want to be known
for my compositions.

for the work that came
from *my heart.*

relief

inspiration

i'm pretty much a firm believer
of learning the best from the worst
from my firsthand experiences.

all the negative experiences
that i come across

are the main reasons
why i decide to write.

and that's what brought
these poems to life.

relief

it's safe to say
that you're gone.

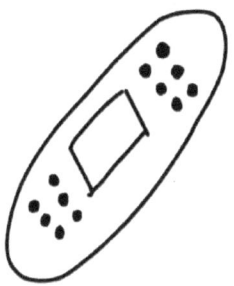

comfort

it's very heartwarming
when you can finally
speak with someone
who relates with you.

who knows how it feels
to be in your shoes.

then you know
you're not in solitude.

where i feel most at peace

bookstores
are my happy place.

i know it sounds unusual,
but they truly are.

i like being surrounded by
the aesthetic environment
of others' creativities.

people who have stories to tell
just like me.

i dodged a bullet

i'm so glad
that i finally got out of
your suffocating energy.

you no longer
have the power
to dominate me.

you no longer
have the power
to treat me
like a fucking pet.

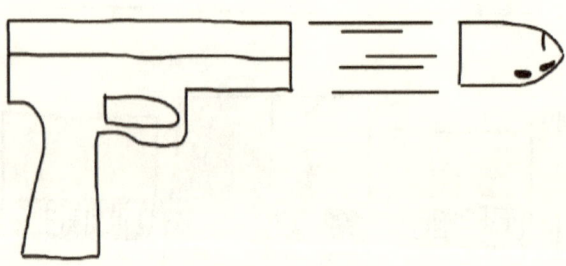

the beauty of writing

if i am ever asked
what i do
to alleviate my suffering,
i will say writing.

whether for poems or for songs,
i always feel the freedom
to express myself
and put all my emotions down
on a simple piece of paper.

this is for me (self-love)

i am what i need.

i am everything i see i could be.

i am the honey to my tea.

no one else defines me
but *me*.

fulfilled

and for once
i can breathe
because i finally had the guts
to share my stories
through these pages
you flipped through.

i can also find peace
in knowing
that someone else
has received the message
this book has to offer.

you are now shining
with the *light.*

and this was all because
we journeyed all the way
from the darkest times of our lives.

we've come a long way.

poems and illustrations by
francesca joanna

ABOUT THE AUTHOR

francesca joanna is an artist and writer born and raised in northern california.

she started reading poetry during her early high school years. after falling in love with poetry, she began to express herself through her first collection, which is her very own *teenage melancholy*. she also had the inspiration to draw and include small illustrations to accompany her poems. francesca aspires to release more poetry collections in the future, sharing her works of art, stories, and messages with the world.

another of francesca's passions includes music. during her leisure time, she enjoys singing covers of popular songs and writing her own original songs. she frequently posts her music on her social media platforms to share this other love of hers with others.

follow the author:
instagram: francescaxjoanna
youtube: francesca joanna
soundcloud: francesca joanna

www.ingramcontent.com/pod-product-compliance
Lightning Source LLC
Chambersburg PA
CBHW022014290426
44109CB00015B/1164